THE STORY
OF THE
FIRST-FIFTH
BEDFORDS

By EDMUND RIMMER

The Naval & Military Press Ltd

Reproduced by kind permission of the Central Library,
Royal Military Academy, Sandhurst

Published by
The Naval & Military Press Ltd
Unit 10, Ridgewood Industrial Park,
Uckfield, East Sussex,
TN22 5QE England
Tel: +44 (0) 1825 749494
Fax: +44 (0) 1825 765701
www.naval-military-press.com
www.military-genealogy.com

© The Naval & Military Press Ltd 2007

The Naval & Military Press ...

...offer specialist books for the serious student of conflict. The range of titles stocked covers the whole spectrum of military history with titles on uniforms, battles, official histories, specialist works containing Medal Rolls and Casualties Lists, and numismatic titles for medal collectors and researchers.

The innovative approach they have to military bookselling and their commitment to publishing have made them Britain's leading independent military bookseller.

In reprinting in facsimile from the original, any imperfections are inevitably reproduced and the quality may fall short of modern type and cartographic standards.

Printed and bound by Antony Rowe Ltd, Eastbourne

FOREWORD.

AS there has been no public record of the history of the battalion in which all the townspeople of Luton are interested, the writer has gathered a few facts which will help to keep green the memory of the 1st Battalion of the 5th Bedfordshire Regiment, not only in our town, but also in the towns and hamlets of the county whose name they have borne with honour.

Some of the incidents are the records sent home by the boys themselves to parents and friends, and for some the writer is indebted to the editors of our local newspapers for their permission to reproduce published reports.

EDMUND RIMMER.

Photo:] [*Bassano Ltd., W.*
LIEUTENANT-COLONEL BRIGHTEN, Commanding Officer, 1/5th Beds.

The Story of the First-Fifth Bedfords.

THE 5th Bedford Regiment (Territorial Force), like many others, had its origin in the Volunteer movement. The Volunteer Regiment, formed in 1869, had its headquarters in Bedford, and consisted of nine companies, of which " C," " F," and " G " Companies were at Luton, the local headquarters being in Park Street. The remaining companies were at Bedford, Ampthill, and in Toddington district. The first uniform was grey, and not a few of the older residents of Luton are well acquainted with the movements of the old volunteers, and ·the popular band which led their marches. Under Lord Haldane's scheme this body became absorbed in the Territorial Force at Bedford—the 1st Battalion consisting of about an equal number of Luton and Huntingdon men, made up to full strength by a few from other companies. Captain Cumberland Brown was the last captain of the volunteers in Luton.

It was early in September, 1914, the word patriotism was impressed on many a brave young heart to which it had previously been a stranger. The old country, which had hitherto merely been a name, became a reality. The mother country ! what was that to them ? The sporting columns of the papers had claimed their first attention. Politics, including military and naval news, never concerned them. Those possessed of real estate or invested wealth might be interested in political affairs, but what were these things to the young men of Luton, whose wealth was the weekly wage and whose only estate what they carried about ? What interest had they in the old country ? Something had happened to command their attention. On this September morning, watching the mixed company of young recruits at the Corn Exchange, one wondered on what common ground such a crowd could meet. Yet here they were, almost as motley a crew as could assemble. Smart young men from the office, well-knit young fellows from the workshops, warehousemen proud of their appearance; others on the pavement, who had never worn a starched collar and had never given a thought to appearance. What was the common ground on which they met? Here was a man leering in the face of the public around him as he joined the increasing company. He could scarcely stand to attention, because he had been "celebrating" the occasion in his customary way of celebrating anything and everything. But he was to be one of their mates; yes, and a worthy mate, too, taking a pride in his appearance and his duty, leaving the dross of his former self, and giving of his best for his country on the sands of Gallipoli, under which he now sleeps. No contempt was shown for the weak one. He was to be one of them—a brother in arms, for he enlisted as they in a common cause. The Kaiser had lit the beacon fires in our land, and our young men were gathering for resistance, determined to stand shoulder to shoulder in the service of their country against a common foe. They marched to the station to entrain for Bedford, to form eventually the 1st Battalion of the 5th Bedfordshire Regiment. Passing through the crowds of onlookers there was a question which forced itself on the crowd. How from this motley throng could a soldiery be formed worthy to meet the highly-trained enemy, and bring credit to our army? Wait and see. There was something hidden in those youths which was to come out in the training. The spirit of the soldier was only dormant. Rough diamonds all; only waiting to be polished to show their worth.

They were sent to Bedford for their early training. I saw them swinging along before they had their khaki,

Photo:] *W. H. Coy, Luton.*
W. J. Primett, Esq., J.P.
Mayor of Luton 1913-14, 1914-15, who welcomed the troops after their long march.

already taking pride in their appearance, looking with some contempt on the slacker and cognisant that they caught the public eye. They made many friends in Bedford, as many a letter which followed them on their journeyings can prove. Friends who followed their movements to far-off Gallipoli, and who sent letters of cheer, of love, fatherly and motherly love, and parcels of comforts showing that the sojourn of our boys in the County town was not forgotten.

Bury St. Edmunds was their next training place, and here came a great physical transition. Here, if the description is permissible, they were sworn at and bullied, and drilled, and sent on their long and trying route marches, ofttimes hungry and thirsty. These were the things which tried and tested them, even disgusted them, till they understood that their officers were getting proud of them, and favourably comparing them with other battalions, till the lads began to be proud of themselves.

At Bury St. Edmunds Cathedral.

Soon after their removal to Bury I saw them marching to the Cathedral. The old veteran, Lord Roberts—the man who had been appealing frantically to the nation to arm and prepare to meet the foe who was secretly preparing to strike a blow at our country—had been called to rest before the great armageddon had awakened his countrymen to a proper appreciation of his devoted efforts and warnings. By some he was considered a dotard; but there were a few men of influence and power who had heeded the warnings, and who silently made preparations which did much to save the national honour. The new battalion attended the memorial service, and heard a touching tribute to the great soldier, and left with a feeling of reverence for the noble patriot who had tried to arouse his countrymen to action.

It was up to them to do their part to stem the torrent which the War-Lord had turned upon their country, and which the departed veteran had predicted. Those were busy times for the battalion at Bury, and our lads were put through it in real earnest. Watching the march past of the new recruits on this Sunday one felt that in some of the platoons there were very youthful elements—below the standard in physique and in age. But there was something very encouraging when one scanned the boys' faces—for many were only boys of seventeen, who in their eagerness to serve had put on several years at a bound, heedless of the calendar or attestation penalties. There was a look of determination which promised much. Anxious they were to bear their part and carry out in detail all that was required of them. Every man was alert, and careful of his appearance. There was already showing in the faces of every company the "pride of regiment" which makes the soldier. Few bestowed even a glance on the friends who were present to watch their parade. The age was sure to come, and the hard training was going to turn the boys into men. Essentials were there—pride, determination, patriotism, giving promise to their officers who saw what was in them—material ready for the moulding.

CHRISTMAS AT BURY.

I saw many of them at Christmas time at the station when the train came in; standing in lines, expectant to meet friends who were visiting them for the "joy of Christmas" and making them feel at home again. The people of Bury St. Edmunds were thoughtful and kind, and crowded themselves out to let the lads have their friends from home; and many a Luton lad felt that life was worth living on that Christmas of 1914, when the friends and relations gathered round and brought to them good cheer, and joined in their songs and merriment in the billets. It was to be the last Christmas gathering for many of them, and that

Photo.] THE MAYORAL RECEPTION AT LUTON. [W. H. Cox, Luton.

thought now and again stole into the minds of both visitor and soldier, but it found no expression among the merry party.

There were some among the lads at Bury who saw little of the joys of Christmas time. There was a row of earnest faces to be seen as you passed along the railway platform to the exit. They had scanned keenly and sadly the faces of each one who passed, expecting a visit from a friend or relation who never came. Lads from poor homes, many of them whose parents could not afford the fares. Perhaps some of them had no friends, but were hoping against hope that they would find some familiar face in this crowd of visitors. There are many such lads in the army; and when the thoughtful, feeling members of the community send comforts to the soldiers, they may often touch the heart of the friendless lad who never gets comforts from home. The boys I visited told me a touching story. They had been to the mess room the day before, hurrying away from parade to join in the scramble for Christmas parcels, which were coming in plentitude. They saw them distributed, and heard the merry laugh and the boyish glee of scores who thought Father Christmas was a jolly old soul because a friendly parcel had come, and they waited and waited till all were given out, and, lo, there were none for them. " It was rotten, I can tell you," said they, " when we had to return to our billets empty-handed. Forgotten at Christmas! It did not seem possible; but there it was, and we wondered that our friends should fail us just now, and we passed the quietest day in billet that we had ever done in our lives."

It was explained afterwards. The traffic had been such that hundreds of parcels did not get through, and were forwarded afterwards to the disappointed lads. " Never mind," they said, " you have made up for it, and we have spent a Christmas in the good old style," and we felt as the lads let themselves go and gave us snatches of their route march songs, and played their tricks on one another, that we had lifted them out of

[*Photo:*] THE 1/5TH BEDFORDS IN FRONT OF THE TOWN HALL AT THE [*Thurston & Son, Luton.*
PUBLIC RECEPTION

the rut and given them something to look back on for many a long day.

Easter came, and I visited them again, and saw them march to a church parade in the fields. They were making progress. Their route marches were making them more fit and strong. They passed along with an easy swinging gait. Where were the undersized lads of a few months ago ? Their training was doing wonders, and they were enjoying it, too. In their sports, organised in friendly rivalry with the lads of neighbouring counties, the boys of the Bedfords easily came out first, and the General gave them praise for their appearance and efficiency on parade.

Two Hundred Volunteers Wanted.

There was some commotion in the camp. A draft was wanted for another regiment which was below its strength, and the 1/5th Bedfords were asked to fill it up by 200 volunteers for active service. The alarm was felt not because they feared active service, but because the proposal to take 200 of their number would destroy their battalion. They were taking an interest in each other, vieing with each other for efficiency. They were *Bedfords*, and desired no other name. What was it to them that another regiment was deficient ? The 1/5th Bedfords were all right, and they refused to be broken up. A call was made for 200 volunteers, and the whole battalion held up their hands. That was the way they defeated the call for men. They were going to face the music all together; whether it was the home service or foreign, there was to be no " separation order " for them.

Prouder than ever were their officers. And the work of training went on more briskly than before, for the lads were in deadly earnest. Intrepid leaders —intrepid soldiers. Their work was full of incident. " Major A will kill every beggar of us," said one of them to me. "He'd make us charge the enemy right through the gap in the hedge where there is

Photo:] AFTER THE RECEPTION. MARCHING THROUGH GEORGE STREET. [W. H. Cox, Luton.

a machine gun fixed. Hope I get out of his squad before we go abroad."

Trying to locate an enemy in the dark, with the feeling that he might be within two yards of you, was a bit trying; but it was more trying still to grope about for a couple of hours after an enemy and then find out that he had retired and was safe in his billet. Of course there were impolite expressions at times, when such accidents occurred.

Bury St. Edmunds was now becoming rather stale to them. They had been marching for more than six months over the same ground day by day, and returning to the same scenes and streets, and so little variety that they were, as they said, "about fed up." "We know every house, every girl, every wall on our route, nearly every tree; we know just how many steps it takes to get to such and such a place, and we are sick of it. The people are all right, but we did not join the army to live and die in Bury St. Edmunds!"

OFF TO NORWICH.

Orders came at length for the desired change, and briskly the boys ran here and there, like schoolboys let out of school, when they learned that Norwich was their destination. It was a sight worth seeing when they all fell in on Easter Monday before marching to their new billeting town. A healthy glow was on every face, a cheery look in every eye, and they stood in their ranks, with their hundred rounds of ammunition and their packs, eager to face the hard march of forty miles, which they were doing in three stages, to the old city, which gave them such a genuine welcome. No body of territorials could have looked more fit, and probably none did more arduous marches than they with fewer "Fall-outs." The boys had become men. There were youthful faces—a goodly number—but the bearing, the confidence, and the alertness was evident in each platoon of the battalion which marched

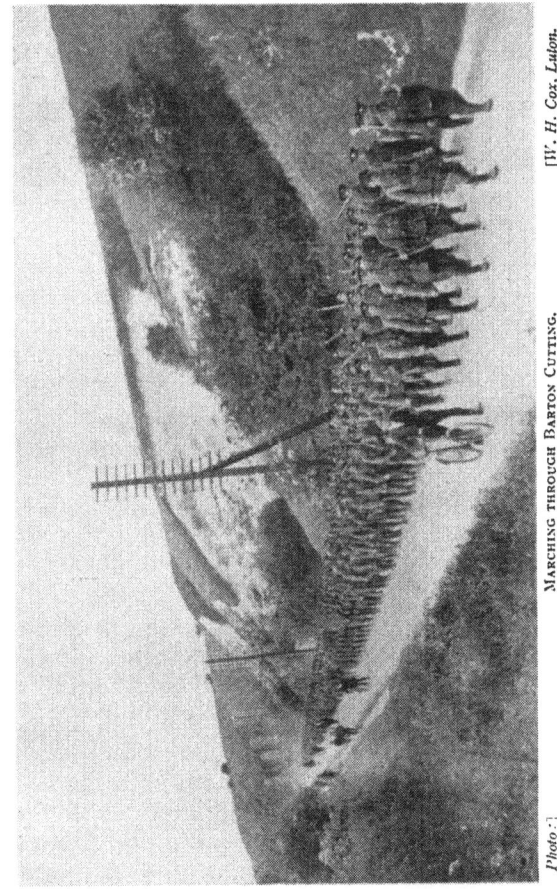

Photo:] MARCHING THROUGH BARTON CUTTING. [W. H. Cox, Luton.

out of Bury St. Edmunds. There were hasty farewells to make, many handshakes to give to the friends they had made, and many a tender look given towards those who were losing a mate who had perhaps been more than a brother to the pale-faced girl who was feeling the parting. Their stay at Norwich was rather short, but long enough to make many friends. The district was new, the city bright and interesting, and the marches through pleasant country. Other soldiers had trained in Norwich, but the citizens gave the Bedfords a special welcome, which touched their hearts and immediately made them feel at home. It was like a holiday, they said; but, more than the change of scene and surroundings, they felt real friendship in their contact with the men, women, and children of Norwich, who seemed to fully appreciate the services these young men were giving to their country. After leaving Norwich they kept in touch with its people, for letters of friendship followed them both to home stations, to Gallipoli, and Egypt. I have seen some of these letters which were sent to the boys by kind fathers and loving mothers, which breathe a pure spirit and tender feeling for boys they might never see again—letters such as fathers and mothers should write to their boys to help them to pursue the noble and true ideal in life. There were mothers who had been by nature denied the voice of boyhood in the home whose hearts were won by the laughter and song of these lads of Bedfordshire, and the boys prized and cherished these messages in their subsequent journeyings, and some of them were left in their keeping on the other side of Suvla Bay, in the land of silence and away from the eye of the stranger.

At St. Albans.

St. Albans was their next and final training station before they went to Gallipoli. They got on well, as usual, and are always spoken of in the highest terms at the cathedral city. There were many

Photo:] TRANSPORT SECTION ON THE WAY TO LUTON. [*W. H. Cox, Luton.*

attractions at St. Albans to break the tedious round of duty, and here the young soldiers seemed without a care in life. Friends from Luton frequently visited them with mutual benefit. But the chief attraction of St. Albans was its proximity to Luton, and when rail and cycle facilities were not available—well, what are ten miles to the young soldier who daily does marches of twelve or fifteen miles with full equipment?

A Peep at the Old Home.

After Sunday church parade dozens would foot it to Luton, swinging along in twos or threes with brisk, soldierly gait, their faces bright with the pleasurable anticipation of seeing home, relations, or friends. They were going to the homes where someone was preparing a good meal for them, and anxious to give them a kindly reception.

They had had their hardest training at Bury, but their officers kept them fit, and many a fine route march was put to their credit around the historical city. It was nice to receive letters from home, to keep in touch with their old friends, to open the parcels which loving friends had sent them, and divide the contents with their pals, but it was nicer still to visit Luton, to see the faces light up with pleasure as they entered the old home, to hear the merry laugh, to be in touch with the home life, to have a square meal provided for them with neither jam nor bully beef in sight.

The home was more to them than it had ever been, because they had not realised its comforts till the floor beds and rough surroundings of camp life initiated them into the hardships of the soldier. There were few expressions of regret that they had left it. Their work was not done—they were ambitious to be doing more. They were said to be attached to a certain division which was waiting its full equipment, and they got restive at the delay, and surprised the officers one day by a deputation stating their grievances—

Part of Anzac Beach, Showing Gaba Tepe and Achi Baba.

A Scene at Lemnos, Where the 1/5th Beds. stayed after leaving the Peninsula.

that they were being kept drilling and "messing about" when they wished to be on active service.

"You ———— fools," the officer is said to have replied. "You don't know what you want. Be content where you are. You will get service enough by and by."

His words no doubt were prophetic, but they did not discourage the eager hearts who felt they were fit for serious work, and they would have repelled the idea to a man of being kept for home defence.

Their Splendid Marches.

A march from St. Albans to Bedford, *via* Houghton Regis (where they stopped for the night), was done in fine style, but the march from Bedford to Luton, a distance of twenty miles on a hot day, with only a single halt for dinner, was the finest on their record. From a battalion nearly 1,000 strong not more than two or three failed to come through fresh and fit. How sprightly their appearance and the healthy glow on their faces as they marched into Luton many of us will never forget. I knew a young soldier who happened to be on leave and standing among the crowd as the battalion arrived. It was interesting to hear his remarks on the fine appearance of the men: "See, not a man out of place. Look at that line there! Perfect, &c.!" He knew the trouble, the training, the dreary repetitions of drill, the weariness of the marches, the exhaustion of patience, the display of temper which had contributed to this fine effect, and his pride of his company was bubbling over because he considered them a force in every way worthy of the honour which was being done to them. The following interesting record of the march is from the *Luton News*:—

THE MARCH.
Reception.

The three days' march from St. Albans *via* Dunstable and Bedford to Luton was a very good test of the men's power of endurance, as they had to cover over 60 miles with full war kit in three days.

View of Malta.

Latter End of Anzac Coast.
1/5th Beds' Landing Place.

The 1/5th Batt. Bedfordshire Regiment, early on Thursday morning, left St. Albans on their march through the county before their departure for the front. They carried full kit, and were, of course, followed by the " kitchens," the cooking being done *en route*. They marched to the music of the band, and passed through Markyate. Near Dunstable they had dinner in Costin's field. There were one or two very welcome visitors from Dunstable in the persons of the Mayor (Councillor F. T. Garrett), the Town Clerk (Mr. C. C. S. Benning), the Rector of Dunstable (Canon Baker), whose son is a second-lieutenant in the battalion, and Mr. Oakley. They were deeply interested with all they saw, and had an enlightening chat with Lieut.-Col. Brighten. By the kindness of these and other friends, the men and officers were provided with liquid refreshments.

Just before dinner Lieut.-Col. Brighten spoke a few words of instruction to the men. He advised them to conduct themselves in accordance with the reputation of the battalion, of which they were very proud.

About 1-30 the battalion moved off to Dunstable, where flags were flying, and where crowds lined the roads ready to welcome the men.

The Mayor said that Dunstable looked upon the 5th Batt. Bedfordshire Regiment as a Dunstable battalion, and they could not let them march through the town without offering them a hearty welcome and congratulation upon their present appearance. They heartily congratulated them on the smartness of their appearance. They knew the battalion had been hard at work to acquire such great efficiency, and they knew from the Commanding Officer that the men had willingly performed their work. They knew that when they were called upon to take a still greater part they would be ready and prepared, and would be anxious to emulate the heroic work of the Bedfordshires now at the front.

Cheers were given for the battalion and Lieut.-Col. Brighten, and the colonel, in responding, said he was proud of his battalion. He expressed thanks for the kindness shown them, and called for cheers for Dunstable.

These the men gave lustily, and afterwards marched off to Houghton Regis for the night.

On Friday the battalion marched from Houghton Regis through Toddington, Westoning, and Flitwick to Ampthill.

At Bedford the battalion was given a civic reception, and a speech, which was very short and quite to the point, was delivered by the Mayor (Mr. H. Browning), whose chapl in also delivered an address of welcome, which was not quite so short.

The battalion then marched round the town, and afterwards to the barracks of the Bedfordshire Regiment, at Kempston, to bivouac for the night in an adjoining field.

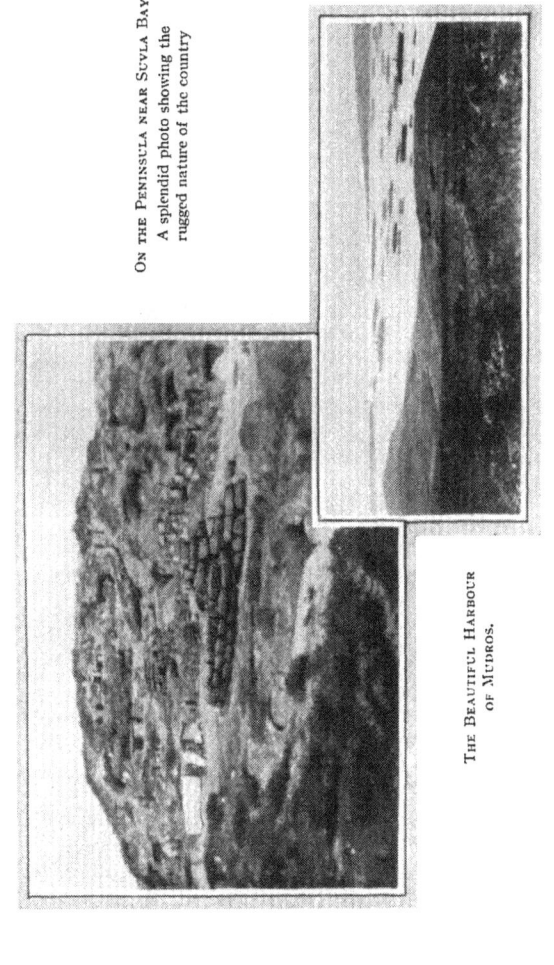

On the Peninsula near Suvla Bay.
A splendid photo showing the rugged nature of the country

The Beautiful Harbour of Mudros.

It should be mentioned that when the men were having dinner, prepared in their own field kitchens on the polo ground, liquid refreshments were provided out of funds subscribed by the townspeople of Bedford, and also smoking material.

There were several distinguished visitors, who occupied specially reserved seats near the flag at the point of salute. The Duke of Bedford, of course, was present on horseback, in khaki, and others present were the Duchess of Bedford, Emily Lady Ampthill, the Hon. Constance Russell, the Hon. Romola Russell, the Lord Lieutenant (Mr. S. Howard Whitbread) and Mrs. Whitbread, and many other distinguished county people.

At 6 a.m. on Saturday, the battalion left Kempston and marched through Clophill and Silsoe to Barton on their way to Luton. They got to Barton at 10-30, and, had it been urgently necessary, could have managed the rest of the journey to Wardown by twelve o'clock, as previously arranged. But having regard to the trying conditions experienced on Friday, and to the heat, Lieut.-Col. Brighten decided in favour of a halt at Barton.

The start from Barton was timed for 4-40. With the usual ten minutes' rest in each hour, this enabled the battalion to get to the Town Hall just in time for the civic reception at 7 p.m. Before they left Barton tea was provided, the menu including bread and butter, cake, and pineapple.

Lieut.-Col. Brighten had with him on the march 20 officers, about 800 men, and 70 horses. The other 15 officers and 200 men were left at St. Albans to continue special courses of instruction which could not be stopped.

The Reception at Luton.

The reception of the battalion at Luton Town Hall on Saturday evening was responsible for a scene unparalleled in the history of the borough. Never before has the whole battalion been seen in the town, and this in itself made it a noteworthy occasion. In addition, there was the probability that it might be the last opportunity Luton would have of seeing the battalion before it went abroad. In these times a battalion is here to-day and gone in the night, and at any moment we may hear that the battalion is no longer in the country. This very fact alone would have justified a demonstration of the popular sentiment, and if any further excuse were needed it was to be found in the fact that the battalion was made up largely of our own men, who came in as a body for the first time since mobilisation, and for the first time under a commanding officer who is also a Lutonian. Lieut.-Col. E. W. Brighten brought his men, who had done a trek of over sixty miles in three hot days, into George Street exactly as the clock was striking seven, and they could not

GHURKAS' RELIGIOUS DANCE.
GROUP OF OFFICERS, 1/5TH BEDS.
A DUG-OUT: "FINSBURY VALE."

have desired a more cordial reception. Chief-constable Teale, Inspector Janes, and other police officers had kept the ground well cleared for the troops, and until the reception by the Mayor and other leading townspeople was over one could hardly tell the size of the crowd which had been drawn together. But when, the troops having resumed their march to Luton Hoo, the public were free to take up the whole roadway, it was really surprising to see what a crowd had gathered to have a first and, maybe, a last, look at the battalion as a whole. Indeed, townspeople able to speak with the authority of long years of experience, said that such a crowd had never before been seen in George Street. We may hope that it will be eclipsed when celebrations mark the return of peace. But be that as it may, Saturday evening's gathering will go down as one of the most memorable occasions in the history of the borough. The Mayor's invitation to residents to decorate their premises was well responded to in the principal thoroughfares, a gay show of flags and bunting being made along the line of route from New Bedford Road to the end of Park Street, and in some of the side streets also.

A temporary platform had been erected outside the Town Hall, and on this the Mayor (Councillor W. J. Primett) was accompanied by various members of the Town Council, the South Bedfordshire Recruiting Committee, and other prominent townspeople. Included were Aldermen T. Cain and H. Arnold, Councillors G. Warren, A. B. Attwood, W. W. Merchant, M. Barford, R. F. Briggs, A. Chapman, S. Green, J. Bone, H. Impey, W. A. Rainbow, J. Unwin, Messrs, J. W. Green, J.P., B. Hartop, H. Inwards (secretary of the Recruiting Committee), T. Keens, C. Cotchin, G. E. M. Walker, F. E. Shoosmith, J. Eaton-Smith, and J. A. Burgess, Rev. G. Roberts Hern, and others. The Mayoress and a number of other ladies had seats at the windows of the Town Hall.

The Mayor, on behalf of the Corporation, Recruiting Committee, and the town generally, gave the battalion a very hearty welcome. They belonged, he said, to a county which had sent out men who had done some wonderful deeds on the field of battle. The Bedfords had accomplished many notable exploits, and had done noble deeds for their country. Probably, in a very short time, this 1/5th Battalion would be called to face the enemy.

"We adore every man of you," said the Mayor, amid cheers, "for the reason that you have voluntarily stepped forward and offered yourselves and your very lives, if need be, to protect our wives and children, and the homes at Luton, of Bedfordshire, and of the country generally." The Bedfords won immortal fame in the heavy fighting of the October-November last, and at Ypres, and again at Hill 60, and they had heard how one of the 1st Bedfords had been decorated

Photo:] OFFICERS OF THE 1/5TH BEDFORDS. [Bassano Ltd., Bond St., W.

for distinguished services. In the last week they had read much of what other boys from Luton had been through. They had heard with joy of boys winning stripes for plucky work on the battlefield, and in the assistance of the wounded, and also with sadness of some who would never return. All honour to the Lutonians and the Bedfordshires! All honour to the men who were making such noble sacrifices!

"Many of you," said the Mayor, "have given up lucrative positions, and broken away from your home circles, to stand in the breach in your country's hour of peril and danger. We honour every one of you. And when you are called upon to meet this most unscrupulous enemy, the vilest enemy that ever fought in battle, I trust you will cherish the thought that we are thinking of you, and that we shall bear you up, not only in our thoughts, but in our prayers also. In the name of every man, woman, and child in Luton, we give you a hearty welcome in our midst, and wish you God speed."

The Mayor complimented the men on their very fit appearance, and said they were all proud of Lieut.-Col. Brighten as commanding officer of the battalion.

Lieut.-Col. Brighten was cheered before replying. He said it would be difficult to express what they all felt at the reception which had been accorded to them. They felt they were at home, and were most gratified at being received in this way. They were proud to belong to the Bedfordshire Regiment, and when their time came they intended to do their part. The men were proud of the battalion. All worked hard and tried to do their best, but the proudest man in the whole battalion was himself.

To show their appreciation of the welcome which had been given, Lieut.-Col. Brighten called for three cheers from the battalion. In a twinkling every man's hat was off, and there was nothing half-hearted about the response. Three cheers for the battalion were then given at the call of the Mayor, and after the band had played the National Anthem the battalion moved off to Luton Hoo.

They bivouacked for the night on the high ground just inside the Park Road entrance to the park, but all men who had homes in the town were given permission to go home for the night, on the condition that they turned up for church parade on the following morning.

For the church parade on Sunday, the Vicar of Luton (the Rev. A. E. Chapman, M.A.) invited the battalion to the Parish Church. The Officers were seated in the choir stalls, as also was the Mayor (who read the lesson) and the Town Clerk, while members of the Recruiting Committee were provided with seats near the chancel steps. Only a few members of the general public were admitted after all the men of the battalion had been accommodated. Mr. F. Gostelow was at the organ, and it was fine to hear the men

CAPTAIN BRIAN C. CUMBERLAND (*Killed in action*).

Captain Cumberland was leading his company, the "A" Company, when he was killed on August 15th, 1915, being given the post of honour in leading the attack. It was his company that advanced farthest and suffered heavily.

sing some of the good old hymns which were included in the order of service.

In his address, the Vicar cordially welcomed the officers and men. He said it was a special gratification to him to find they were prepared to come to that historic church once more before passing to France or to whatever their destination might be. Not only was the Luton Parish Church a house of God, but it was a place worthy for soldiers to worship in, as it was really built by soldiers. In 931, Athelstan, the King, and one of the best soldiers of his time, was there for the dedication of the church. Then in 1120 Robert, Duke of Gloucester, one of the best soldiers of his day, really built the greater part of the church, and it was to him they could look back when they thought about this splendid house of God. In 1461 the first Lord Wenlock, who was slain in the Wars of the Roses, built the latest part of the church, the Someries Chapel, which had been recently restored so beautifully by Lady Wernher. It was a soldiers' church, and the spirit of those splendid warriors, who did their duty to the country in the days that were past, still lived in our midst. In these later times there was the same keen spirit of determination to stand up for God, for King and country, and to see to it that the British Empire never suffered for want of the duty and loyalty of her sons. Luton was proud of the 1/5th Battalion, and whenever they were mentioned one heard how splendidly fit the men were.

On leaving the church, the battalion marched through some of the principal streets. They were then dismissed at the Corn Exchange, and were free until the evening, when they had to parade at Luton Hoo and march back to St. Albans.

THE DEPARTURE.

July 25th, 1915, was a busy and exciting day. It was their last day in the old country. As they marched to the old Abbey in the morning the crowds turned out to bid them farewell. It was a hearty service in which they joined, and right heartily they sang the popular hymns. The battalion was fond of singing, and one could always hear the popular airs in various sections of the line on the march. After service they formed up in the field near the church, and Lieut.-Col. Brighten, following their movements, was evidently proud of his men. The service over, they went back to their billets for their last dinner in old England, at any rate for many a long day. Later

c

the city was all animation. The lads had got their sun helmets on, and had a changed appearance.

It was interesting to see the scores of mules being hustled by their drivers in and out of the various quarters, and to see the men in the streets with loads of equipment on the ground trying to find space for it. There were hand-shakes later on, and many hearty wishes for the safe return of the lads who had made so many friends, and who were going out to face unknown risks in a land of disease and death. There were secret little meetings, where the hearts were strangely sad—fathers, mothers, and sisters who held the arms of their boys tightly for a little space because the fear came into their hearts that they might not see them again.

In the dead of night the lads trooped down to the station, and early on the morning of the 26th they left the station with many a good wish for their welfare. The voyage was a pleasant one, and the diary of one of their number, my son, Pte. Frank Rimmer, gives an interesting account of the voyage to Alexandria.

The stay at Alexandria was very brief. It was believed that the boys would stay here for some days, if not weeks, to acclimatise. An old friend who had spent some years in Egypt assured me that the army authorities *must* give them some weeks to get used to the very trying climate, as the lads would not be fit for their arduous task otherwise. *Must* is a potent word, but the need of their help in the great task was more potent still, and the dreams of seeing the wonders of this fabled land were dispelled, and one short march was all they got in the land of the Pharaohs. It was a march many of them will remember for its glimpse of the old time city, but, it left them no time to pick up the relics or wonderful knick-knacks of the ancient people which they had promised to their home friends. On they pressed, and even letters and parcels from home could not overtake them in this hurried voyage, and many a young heart was aching for messages from home, which were long delayed. Some, indeed, never

Photo :] [H. J. Jarman & Co., Bury St. Edmunds.
CAPTAIN SHOOSMITH (*Killed in Gallipoli*).

The report of August 15th, 1915, says Shoosmith had a charmed life that day. Practically all his N.C.O.'s and men were knocked out, and he was left only with one man to fight his gun, which he did with the utmost gallantry. He swept the ground clear for our advance.

were delivered, being returned to the sender with sad messages from those whose duty it was to break the saddest of news to the relatives. By-and-by this confusion was remedied, and those who were fortunate enough to receive parcels rejoiced in the remembrance of their friends and kindred, and life, even amid the trials of such a climate, was still worth living.

Photo :] SEC.-LIEUT. R. D. J. BRIGHTEN. [*"Luton News.'*
(*Killed in action, August 15th, 1915*).

His body was found three days afterwards with a number of his fallen men around him. He had advanced with his platoon to the farthest point reached in the action.

The following diaries of my son, Pte. F. Rimmer, and his mates, Ptes. Goodwin and Scott, give records of the daily work. The first shows the longing for home creeping in on the voyage when the thoughts of the welcome home are stirred by the words of the "Little Grey Home in the West." It was a welcome which was never experienced, for the writer shared the fate of many of his brave mates of " A " Company who advanced into the deadly area of the Turkish shells on August 15th. He was afterwards found close to Sec.-Lieut. R. D. J. Brighten, and buried with him near the One Tree Valley.

DIARY OF OUTWARD VOYAGE.

S.S. " Bræmar Castle,"
Sunday Evening, August 1st, 1915.
Mediterranean Sea
(In sight of the Algerian Coast).

DEAR DAD AND MA,

I am hoping you will get this letter safely when the ship returns to England, as it is going to be posted there, if possible. We left St. Albans in the early morning of Monday, July 26th, and passed through Reading, Swindon, Bath, Bristol, Exeter (where we received tea, sandwiches, cigarettes, &c., with the Mayor's compliments), and then to Devonport, where the train took us alongside our liner, and we embarked immediately. At tea time we sailed, and sat till dusk watching the old land fade away. Down below on our troop deck we had tea, slung our hammocks, jumped into them, and soon were sound asleep. At 5-30 on Tuesday we "showed a leg" (the sailors' term for tumbling out of his hammock), and found we were out of sight of land. We had plenty to do during the day, including stowing away rifles and helmets, and had kit and boat drill. This is our menu: For breakfast we have a plate of porridge, a bloater, and bread and butter and tea. Dinner time: Potatoes and beans, and every other day plum duff or rice pudding. Tea: Bread, butter, and jam; and the cooking is A1. We buy extras from the canteen, and live very well.

Photo:] *Bassano Ltd., Bond St., W.*
CAPT. BAKER
(*Killed in action, September 15th, 1915, son of the Rector of Dunstable*).
Although suffering from a shattered arm he went on at the head of his company until he was shot again.

The Story of the First-Fifth Bedfords. 41

On Wednesday everybody was practically better, and we had an hour's physical drill, boat drill, and did as we liked the rest of the day, with a sing-song on deck in the evening.

Thursday found us still at sea, and at each end of the ship a big sheet was filled with water, and made a bath about a foot deep. I went on guard on Thursday night, watching for submarines. It was a lovely moonlight night, and we could see very clearly. We came off at 5 a.m.; the only incident was some of the crew came washing the deck down with a hosepipe, and didn't see the relief party lying asleep on the deck. They woke up in a tremendous hurry, and thought the ship was sinking. We were still out of sight of land, the reason being that we had made a big sweep out in the Atlantic to avoid traffic. We passed Gibraltar at 11-30 p.m., and, of course, did not see the rock, as it was misty. The fog horns were going all night, and we heard in the morning that we were within a few hundred yards of ramming the "Mauretania," returning home.

The morning of Saturday, July 31st, still found us at sea, and we had the usual drills during the day. We began to feel the heat now, but not being overworked we managed to exist.

Sunday morning, August 1st.—To-day we found we were in sight of the Algerian coast. We could see the mountains rising out of the sea 50 miles away. Church parade was held on deck by the chaplain, and after that we had the day to ourselves. A French destroyer came right up to us and wished us *bon voyage*, and in the evening Brigadier-General de Winton held a service on deck, and had a big congregation. Then we turned in at 8 p.m. I jumped out at 4 a.m. on Bank Holiday Monday and had a lovely bath. We had drill and a medical inspection, and we finished for the day. We are running within a few miles of Algeria. Rocky mountains run right into the sea, with here and there the shining white towns with dome house tops. It is a beautiful picture. The sea has hardly a ripple, and there is a bright blue sky. No clouds can be seen, and the sun is almost right overhead. To the north we passed several rocky islands, apparently not inhabited. Nothing further occurred of any note, and we turned in at 7 p.m. During the night the sea rose a bit, and several chaps who slept near the port holes got a beautiful bath free of charge. I am writing this part about two hours' sail from Valetta (Malta). The boys are all on deck singing " Little Grey Home in the West," to the accompaniment of a mandoline and flute, and it makes me long for the day when " Hands will welcome me in " to my Western home again.

We arrived at Malta at 10 a.m. on Tuesday, August 3rd, and anchored in the beautiful harbour of Valetta at 1 o'clock. We were at once surrounded by hundreds of little boats carrying fruit (which we were not allowed to buy), tobacco, shawls, and all kinds of fancy articles. Little brown boys dived for money, and it made a picture to be remembered. The harbour is very heavily fortified, and contained many British and French warships and transports. We got no chance to get ashore, but lay very close to the town, and could see the square houses and narrow streets. But our stay was short, and here we are again at sea, and steaming east. The beautiful island is just fading away over a calm sea. It has been awfully hot to-day, but we are getting used to it. The band is playing " Till the Boys Come Home," and I think I will just join them in the sing-song till lights-out.

Wednesday, August 4th.—We are quite out at sea and have not seen a ship at all. It has been an uneventful day—nothing to do but read. I have written you a post card to-day to go off at Alexandria, but, of course, there is not much on it, as the officers censor our letters. It has been very hot again with a calm sea.

Thursday, August 5th.—I am having to finish up now, as there is a risk that we may have to leave the ship in a hurry at Alexandria to-morrow, and I must

CAPTAIN F. V. ANDREINI

This gallant officer with his platoon took part in the fight, and was at first reported missing. He had a slight sunstroke, but afterwards rejoined his regiment.

The Story of the First-Fifth Bedfords. 45

give this in. I hope it will reach you safely sometime or other, and will be more interesting than the usual post cards.
So good-bye for the present. With fondest love from your loving boy,
FRANK.

A diary by Pte. Harold Scott brings the battalion to the scene of action, and one by Pte. H. Goodwin records the work from the landing to the morning of the 15th August.

DIARY OF PTE. H. SCOTT.

You had most of the details from Frank's letter, I think, covering the period from leaving England until we arrived at Alexandria on Saturday, August 7th. We had a route march round the city, and embarked again for the Peninsula in the evening. I well remember the church service we had the next morning, when Brigadier-General de Winton addressed us and conducted the service. He finished up with the words, "We are going into a strange land to fight our country's battles, and many of us may fall, but I hope the great majority will soon be back in our own homes again, enjoying peace and quietness, which I pray to God may soon rest upon the world."

Tuesday, August 10th.—We arrived at Mudros in the morning, leaving late in the day and going into Imbros for the night. We left again before dawn, and early on August 11th we were making preparations to land at Suvla Bay, which landing had been partly made by the 10th (Irish) Division four days previously. Once ashore—we had very little difficulty in managing that—we went about half a mile inland and deposited our goods and chattels in practically open country. It did not take us long to realise that we were at last on Active Service—too active for us in matters of fatigue duty, &c., and shortly we had our first sample of "iron rations"—bully beef and biscuits. We turned into our blankets as soon as it was dusk, and I believe slept soundly, in spite of the fact that the Turks were endeavouring to shell our ships, whilst our batteries and naval guns were answering frequently.

Thursday, August 12th.—An easy day for us, with nothing to do but cook food, fetch water, write letters, and go bathing.

Friday, 13th.—Found us trench digging in the morning and afternoon, which proved rather exciting. We were making second line trenches, and occasionally we were treated to a few rounds rapid from somewhere in front, but fortunately none was hurt until we were coming back, when one officer and a man got hit. While we were making the trenches, Frank did all the shovel work while I used the pick.

Saturday, 14th.—We rested most of the day, while in the afternoon the General of the Division made a speech to us. In the evening we were again out with the intention of finishing the trenches, but we did not make much progress owing to the severe peppering we had from the Turks. Most of the time we lay huddled behind the earth we had thrown up before, and early in the morning, almost tired out, we returned to our lines and tried to sleep.

Sunday, 15th, was the *day* for our battalion, when great yet terrible things happened. I have only a hazy idea of what happened after Frank and myself returned from scouting on the right.

VOLUNTEERS WANTED.

Pte. Scott then alluded to an incident which took place just previous to the advance of " A " Company. Captain Cumberland had called for two volunteers to scout to the right previous to the advance, so that they should not be surprised by the enemy at close quarters. Pte. Scott and Pte. Rimmer had volunteered, and Pte. Scott gives the following version of the incident :—

We had already missed Nobbie, and soon Frank went on in front of me as we were climbing the hill, on the top

Photo:] [Speight & Co., New Bond Street, W.

CAPTAIN WALTER MEAKIN

(*Reported missing; believed killed August 15th, 1915*).

He was the leader of "C" Company, which supported "B" in the attack. A comrade says: "I am told he was hit, but the man who saw it was hit himself later. We never found him, though we spent nights of searching.'

of which I found Captain Cumberland and one or two more of the boys.

Since we (himself and Pte. Rimmer) managed to get billeted together at St. Albans we stuck fast, and were hardly out of each other's sight until that never-to-be-forgotten day on the Peninsula. It was a terrible day, made worse because we really did not know that we were going into the thick of it until it came on us with frightful suddenness. Then we realised that anyone who came out of it untouched would be indeed lucky. As usual, our company ("A" Company) got into the thick of it, and out of our platoon, which Captain Cumberland was leading, only five were present at roll call when sent back for a rest. While we were advancing up the hill (on August 15th) Captain Cumberland asked for two volunteers to go out and make sure that there was no chance of us being attacked on the right flank. I had my back turned at the time, but, of course, looked round to see what would happen, and almost expected to see Frank's hand shoot up, and sure he was the first to volunteer. It was just like him—he had no fear—and I naturally wanted to be with him in the sport, so I said I would go too. We had rather an exciting time, as the bullets were coming around us pretty thickly, but nothing else happened. When we got back our chaps were just going up the hill in fine style, and in the excitement I lost sight of Frank, as he was running on. He could run faster than me, and that was the last I saw of him. Directly afterwards I came across the captain and got mine in the foot.

PTE. GOODWIN'S DIARY.

At the Peninsula.

We reached Suvla Bay on August 10th, 1915, and anchored for the night. Our first experience of war came very early next morning, one of the enemy aeroplanes coming over and dropping a few bombs between the ships in which we were, but luckily none were hit. We rushed on deck to have a look at them. Of course, it was the worst thing we could have done, but you can guess how we were, and wanted to see all, and I can tell you we saw some very good firing from our guns. They *did* let him have it hot. Shrapnel went all round him and he soon had to retire, but we were all eager to see another one come over to have a little more excitement. After that we went down and had breakfast, and then we got our things together ready for landing. We left our large boat and entered the small boats, on which we were simply packed, and, to make matters worse, it was a very hot day. Well, I suppose we felt it more, going straight there, but we got along somehow to our resting place, which I should say was about a mile from the beach. We landed without a shot being fired, so we were very lucky in that way. We had no sooner got to our rest camp than they started us to work, some unloading the boats, others on water fatigue. I was on the water fatigue, filling tins and skins (the old water bottles of the Jews), to go on mules, and we quite thought we had to go up to the firing line with this water, as the lieutenant told us the poor chaps in the trenches had not had any water for twenty-four hours, and we had to hurry and get it up there. However, the Indians took the water up; each Indian had four mules to look after (and some of them wanted looking after, too). If one mule happened to touch another there was a mess-up; they kicked and jumped, and were not satisfied until they had thrown everything off their backs, and we had the job of putting the load all up again. For the rest of the day we were getting food ready, and then went for a bathe. The bathing was a bit of a luxury, as the water was warm, and you could stay in any length of time without discomfort. There was one drawback to the bathing, as enemy shells were passing over our heads, and our own ships were giving exchange. We had not been in the neighbourhood long, but we were getting used to the shells, and did not duck and dodge about as we had done at first. After the bathing we

Photo:] [H. J. Jarman & Co., Bury St. Edmunds.
LIEUT. C. R. LYDEKKER, The Lodge, Harpenden
(*Killed in Action August 15th, 1915*).
A gallant officer beloved by his men.

came back and drew rations, and got ready for the night's rest. We had two blankets, and lay down and had a quiet night.

On the morning of the 12th we got our little fires on the go, and soon had our breakfast; then cleaned our rifles and had an inspection and another bathe, and then had to line up to fetch water. Two men out of each platoon were told off for this, and it was awful to see the eagerness of hundreds of men waiting for their turn for water, and we were only allowed to take our water bottles. If we wanted to take a large tin to fill, we had to get a note from the officer before we could fill it. After this business we got dinner, and then had the excitement of seeing the Turks firing on our ships, and they let them have it rather hot. Our ships kept on the move during the firing, and then began to let them have it back and silenced them. We were near the coast and in a line with the ships, but, fortunately, they did not get among us, and we had a quiet day and a quiet night, too.

On the next day, August 13th, we went through the same orders as the day before, but at dinner time we knew that the Turks had got our position, for they started shelling us, as we were on open ground. The ravines and gulleys were behind us, where we could have got some shelter, but our colonel told us he was awaiting orders whether we had to dig in there, or in a safer spot further back. Some of the battalions were already on the work, but our orders came along soon, and I can tell you we were not long before we made some cover, and the shells seemed to go over our heads or drop short, so we had no casualties. Being our first experience, we did a bit of bobbing up and down when we heard a shell coming, and as soon as we heard it go over, it was a picture to see all our heads bob up to look where it was bursting. I will say they caught the Indians and the mules which were just behind us one nasty smack, and they cleared off in surprisingly quick time. After about an hour the shelling stopped, and it was safe for us to lie outside our dug-outs. As the sun was hot we generally fixed a bit of shade up with our blankets and rifles, and they made a sort of tent. That night we had orders to go trench digging, and I should think we went a good two or three miles, but it is hard to judge distances in the dark, over rough and uneven ground. " A " and " B " Companies went first, " C " and " D " Companies following, as if in fighting order, and with pick or shovel we marched along, and the snipers were all over the place. The companies following us had an easy time, as they returned without much digging. I suppose we did what was required. I think we were very lucky, for " B " Company did not have one hit, but " A " Company had one hit in the foot by a sniper as we were returning up a gully.

On the morning of the 14th " C " and " D " Companies went up, but they were not so lucky as our company had been, and they had a fair number wounded. We were resting till dinner time, when the Turks let us have it again, to show they were alive, and so we had to get on with our dug-outs. At night we went up again, but this time we were not so lucky, as we had some wounded as soon as ever we got to our trenches. The snipers were very hot, bullets coming from all directions; but we stuck to our work, and were relieved after about two hours' hard digging. We had a little rest in the morning, cleaned our rifles, &c., and then we went and had our bathe, and after drawing rations for the day had a quiet morning. We were just settling down to dinner when we had orders to hurry up and have dinner and draw rations for three days—corned beef and biscuits. Our lieutenant came up and told us to take as many rations as we could, as we were going up in the communication trenches for three days. He said it was a snip job, and, by jove, it was ! Some of us carried tins of water, besides 250 rounds of ammunition and rifle and rations, so you can tell we were fairly loaded.

Captain Cumberland and the "A" Company at Bury St. Edmunds.

INTO THE FIGHT.

They were now entering on their first battle, of which the following narrative from the *Luton News* is a fine description:—

The battalion, after leaving Alexandria, which was only touched for the purpose of landing reserves of about 170 men, sailed across the Mediterranean and were landed " somewhere " on the shore of the Gallipoli Peninsula. In the words of one who took part in the landing, " they fell right into it straight away," for in fact the Bedfordshire lads found there was not much in distance between them and the enemy.

On the shores while landing, and on the beach when camped, the Turks had found the artillery distance and dropped shells into the men during various times of the day. Although the shell fire was accurately distanced and timed, the damage done was extraordinarily small, and this has continued to be, at all events, up to the middle of September, the experience of our battalion.

As soon as the stores were landed all hands were set to dig themselves in, and during this necessary operation the enemy opened a long range musketry fire, accompanied at intervals with shrapnel. The " baptism of fire " to lads who had never been under fire before, all of them only a few months before sitting calmly in offices, working at the bench, or steadily engaged on some agricultural work, must have been a distinct nerve-shaker. But an eye-witness says: " It was perfectly wonderful to see the men going on coolly with their digging just as if they had been at home."

It was during these first two days that the regiment experienced its first casualties. Among them was Lieut. Chaundler, of Biggleswade, but so steady was the discipline that although wounded he just sat down and went on directing his platoon until it was insisted upon that he should retire to the rear.

As an example, however, of the enemy's shell firing it may here be mentioned that while supervising and assisting the men during these entrenching operations, no less than three shells burst within a few feet of Lieut.-Colonel Brighten.

On Sunday, the 15th, the battalion was ordered into action. The general position of the brigade cannot, of course, be given here for obvious reasons, but the 1/5th had to act as a flank guard to a division which was making a push to straighten out the line. The battalion was given the post of honour in the van of the brigade. " B " Company, under the command of Capt. Baker (son of the Rector of Dunstable), was put on the right flank of the battalion, to keep in touch with the other troops; " A " Company, under the command of Capt. Brian Cumberland (son of Mr. Hugh Cumberland, of Luton), was

PRIVATE FRANK RIMMER (*Killed in action, August 15th, 1915*).
The writer of the diary of the voyage, and one of the volunteers asked for by Captain Cumberland. His mate's letter says: " The Captain called for volunteers. I saw Frank's hand shoot up. It was just like him; he had no fear. So I said I would go too."

extended back a little on the dangerous flank that had to be most carefully watched, and the machine gun section, under Lieut. Shoosmith, was detailed to support " A " Company.

The battalion, at the time of the attack, besides those left at Alexandria, was short of one platoon of men and one machine gun section, both of which had to be left to garrison the trenches the battalion had been digging. Lieut. Woodhouse was in charge of that party. The regimental headquarters section followed the two leading companies, and the reserve companies, " C " and " D ", under Captains Meakin and Forrest respectively, were close behind. The following diagram will give some little idea as to the disposition of the battalion :—

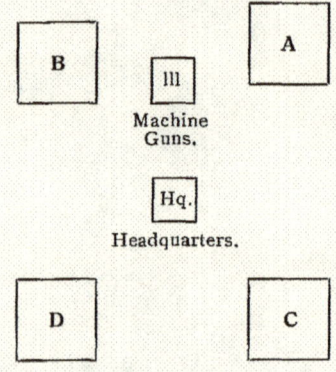

Very soon a message was delivered saying that the hill in front was very strongly held, and then the battalion " went for it." " C " Company was thrown forward with " A " and " B " Companies, and the three companies at once very hotly engaged in the attempt to clear the hill. It was not long before " D " Company had to be thrust onwards to support the charge. This weight of brave, intrepid, well-disciplined men soon took the first hill, but the next proved a much more difficult proposition.

The nature of the country in Gallipoli is such that any exact account of what subsequently happened is impossible, the small precipitous hills, the immense boulders of rock, and the tangled thickets of scrub—the two latter features naturally taken all possible advantage of for cover—make an observer's chances very small, and it is only from piecing various accounts from all quarters together that any choate idea can be formed as to the " carry on " of the movement.

These obstacles, in themselves formidable enough, against observation were aided by the fact that at the assault of the second hill the tide of battle seemed to run off very much from

PRIVATE HORACE GOODWIN.
Writer of diary from the landing to the action of August 15th, 1915.

PRIVATE HAROLD SCOTT.
One of the Volunteers wanted by Captain Cumberland. He was afterwards wounded and invalided home.

the region of the Bedfords' headquarters, and it became very difficult to keep in touch with the various units.

The Adjutant, Capt. Younghusband, and Major Hill, were here of the greatest assistance to Lieut.-Col. Brighten, and hurried from place to place under a searching fire, assisting to get the direction of attack changed, and to keep the four companies in touch with each other. They must have borne charmed lives, for how they got through without a scratch it is impossible to explain.

When once more the battalion was in touch and moved forward it came suddenly into a zone swept by an enfilade of shrapnel fire. This enfilade had evidently been carefully prepared, as the enemy's infantry immediately cleared off the slopes of the hill, leaving the operations to the artillery. Shell after shell fell into the Bedfords, some dropped on top of the Headquarters Section, and the place became a shambles. Lieut. Ballance, of Dunstable (Lieut.-Col. Brighten's signal officer), was wounded at this period, and Lieut. Hunter passed, being taken to the rear with a shrapnel wound in the foot. All the wounded men seemed to crawl towards headquarters, and for some time came so thickly one could hardly move.

This was a time to rack the nerves of any officer. Men who had passed through previous campaign and with nerves of steel might view such a sight with calmness, but our boys, at this first sign of the effects of modern warfare, might have been excused had their steadiness deserted them. But what really happened? Instead of shrinking, the sight rather braced up their strength, for they knew that the best way to protect their wounded was to keep the line whole and preserve the ground which they had taken.

Once more the units of the battalion were brought into touch, casualties were sorted out, and the attack was continued. About this time news came that the Brigadier-General, General C. de Winton, had been wounded. This very gallant gentleman had endeared himself to every officer and man in his Brigade, and although he and some of his staff officers were wounded, remembering the straits of the 1/5th Bedfordshires, he ordered up two more battalions to support them.

The day was now waning and the work was not done, but the attack carried the Bedfords to the crest of the second hill, where both musketry and machine gun firing was terrific.

Capt. Baker, although suffering from a shattered arm, went on at the head of his company until he fell, shot again. Lieut. Lydekker, of Harpenden, was also killed in this assault. "Cumberland," we are told by an eye witness, "called on his Company (" A ") for the last charge up the crest, and in the act of waving them on was shot through the head; Lieut. Ralph (the brother of Lieut.-Col. Brighten), who led No. 1 Platoon of " A " Company, which was poor Cumberland's show platoon, was close to him, and was shot almost at the same

Sergeant W. Stapleton, Ampthill. Sergeant T. Billing, Wootton.
Lance-Sergeant J. A. W. Robinson, Ampthill.
Private C. A. Finch, Private G. Diemer,
98, High Street, Dunstable. Beaconsfield Road, Bedford

KILLED IN ACTION.

time; Lieut. Rising (who has since been reported 'wounded and missing') was not seen after this charge, and has never been found, so it is believed, too, that he is killed."

What a glorious charge! But what a price to pay, for this list of officers did not exhaust the casualties. Lieut. James (Mrs. Brighten's brother) was wounded very early in the action, being shot in the calf of the leg, but he was able to hobble back by himself during the night. The leader of " C " Company, which had supported " B " Company in the attack, Capt. Meakin, is believed to have been killed at this time. A comrade says:—" I am told he was hit, but the man who saw it was hit himself later; we never found him either, although I personally spent nights of searching."

Lieut. Day was also wounded badly in the head, but, like the rest of the cheerful Bedfords, made very light of it. Lieuts. Chirnside and Yarde were hit about this time, too, but went on, not only during the remainder of that attack, but also through the next day and night until relieved.

Although one records these facts with sorrow, yet one is bound to feel pride in conduct like this. These two young officers, when night fell, " found that their company was in for another 24 hours' shift, and insisted on stopping. Brave lads, both of them." It was not until Tuesday night, when they were seen by the doctor, that they could be induced to leave and be packed off to hospital.

" D " Company had, during the attack, supported " A " Company, and being the last company to be brought up had fared a little better, although they had been badly wanted. Capt. Forrest opened an old wound early in the day, and his junior, Capt. Andreini (well known to all Luton straw traders), got a touch of sunstroke. Apart from these the casualties were all in the rank and file.

Here must be quoted another communication, also relative to the fight of the 1/5th. " Shoosmith bore a charmed life that day. Practically all his N.C.O.'s and men were knocked out, and he was left with only one man to fight his gun, which he did with the utmost gallantry; and he simply swept the ground in front of our advance and cleared the way for them."

During the above-mentioned single handling of the gun Major Hill, seeing it was a very pressing moment, and fearing the worst, went up to Lieut. Shoosmith (the son of Mr. Frank Shoosmith, of Luton) and asked him, " Who is to fight the gun if you get knocked out ? No one else knows enough about it up here; your section is gone, and you had better show me how to do it." The answer was, " Oh, you just pull this and press that; it's quite simple ! " All the time this was going on Lieut. Shoosmith was letting the gun rip into the Turks for all he was worth.

Night fell just as the summit was won, and found the remnants of three battalions in a very mixed-up condition

SERGEANT F. BUTLER, Potter's Cross, Wootton.
PRIVATE H. WARDLE, Caddington.
PRIVATE A. WOODCROFT, Flitwick.
PRIVATE HAROLD QUICK, Leighton Buzzard.
PRIVATE G. STOKES, 20, King's Road, Kempston.

DIED OF WOUNDS

around the top of the hill. Although desperately weary, the men had to entrench themselves and hold the line in a fairly straightened manner. Adjt. and Capt. Younghusband ran about and collected all the " bits " of platoons left, and made some sort of a line, and Major White took charge of the advanced units. The Headquarters were established in a small way in a fold of the ground about 50 yards behind the line, and there men were collected and organised for fatigue parties, to fetch up, first of all, tools and sandbags and barbed wire, then food and water. Owing to the circumstances that night there was no surplus of either of the latter articles.

While this was being done by some sections, others were collecting the wounded and bringing them to the Headquarters Section, where they awaited the field ambulance, which during the night managed to get them all away.

At dawn, on Monday, August 16th, more entrenchments had to be made, and the Headquarters was then fixed up in a sort of natural ditch or gully that the Colonel had said " he had had his eye on," and then the section set to work to dig and fortify it partly as headquarters and partly as a support trench. A telephone wire was also run out and the Brigade Headquarters brought into touch. These operations were carried out with the utmost rapidity, for one knew that immediately it was light enough the enemy would start shelling the position.

Soon shrapnel shells were bursting all around. This fire went on all day in the endeavour of the Turks to get the Bedfords out, but they were far too snugly ensconced and far too wary and brave to lose what they had gained at such a cost.

During the day Lieut. Rawlins, seeing a wounded Bedford lying in front, left the trenches to bring him in. While engaged in this merciful errand he himself was wounded, and had to be brought in after a time by another brave man, Pte. Bell, who since has been promoted to Co-Qmr.-Sgt. Again during this day Lieut. Shoosmith held things together with his gun, and any movement of the Turks towards the Bedford lines was countered by him at once.

The night of Monday was comparatively peaceful, and men of the battalion have said how thankful they were for the nights of calm. " The days were all too long and the nights all too short," writes one wearied officer. But even the nights were not all rest. They were partly taken up with digging and re-organisation, and on Monday night the first proper re-organisation of the battalion took place. The companies were arranged into a battalion frontage, " A " and " B " Companies were withdrawn from the front line and set to make some reserve trenches a little behind the Headquarters. During this night, too, all the gallant dead were reverently laid to rest. And so another night passed !

The next day was very like the preceding, except that by now the battalion could report by telephone the effect and

SERGEANT ALBERT PAYNE,
   2, Beech Road, Luton.
SERGEANT W. H. FOSTER,
   Flitwick.
SERGEANT A. HINKS,
   32, Windsor Street, Luton.
CORPORAL N. PAYNE,
   2, Beech Road, Luton.

KILLED IN ACTION.

range of the fire of our own artillery, and help them to get the exact position of the Turks, and the comparative calm enabled the regiment to dig itself deeper in.

On Tuesday night " A " and " B " Companies were put back in the trenches, and " C " and " D " Companies were taken out for 24 hours. This operation was repeated as each day went on, and gradually the battalion got more comfortable; more troops also were sent up to the front, and this went on until Friday, the 20th, when another forward movement was undertaken in another part of the line, but which, of course, had to be supported by fire by the 1/5th Bedfords.

Naturally this drew fire in return, and it was during such a comparative calm that Lieut. Shoosmith got hit and killed. It is said he was walking from one part of the trench to another, when by his height his head was exposed and a bullet struck him. We have it on the best of evidence that on learning of his death, Col. Brighten exclaimed that he had " lost a tower of strength."

On the Sunday following more fresh troops came up during the night, and the Bedfords were relieved and sent down to their old camp, where they could bathe in the sea and bask in the sun to their heart's content. They loved the bathing, but they were quite prepared to do with a little less sun, and the beach presented a most eccentric appearance, for wherever they could be installed, blankets were stretched to give some kind of shade. About this time Capt. Maier had been feeling seedy with dysentery and had to go to hospital, and on the Sunday the reserve left at Alexandria, under Capt. Smythe and Lieut. Hobbs, was landed as a reinforcement.

" After that," says another letter, " we had a day or two's rest, or at least what is called a rest out here; there's always a number of fatigues to be done, and always the shell fire to dodge. We were then sent into another part of the line, where we now are, and where we spend six days in the trenches and six out. When we are out we get back a little behind the line, still under rifle fire, and we find digging parties (every man doing six hours a day in addition to his ordinary battalion routine) to work up in the trenches and on the communications behind."

Adjt. Younghusband was next day wounded in the knee, but fortunately not very seriously. Lieut. Woodhouse was slightly wounded in the arm, and Capt. Smythe was shot in the head and never recovered consciousness, dying next morning.

FOR LOVE OF A PAL.

It was a few days after the fateful 15th, when the gallant lads who had never returned were interred in their last sacred dwelling-place, that a lad of the "A" Company sought one of the R.A.M.C. men and made inquiries as to the place where his

LANCE-CORPORAL ROLAND ABBOTT,
77, Chase Street, Luton.
PRIVATE L. HURD,
32, Beech Road, Luton.
PRIVATE WILLIAM JARVIS,
Dorset Street, Luton.
PRIVATE F. W. THURLOW,
216, Wellington Street, Luton.
DIED OF WOUNDS.

mate had been found. He was missing his mate, for they had been more or less together since they went to Bedford, and now he felt as if he should at least like to see the exact spot where he lay, so that he could fix his mind in years to come on this far-away grave among the rocks of the Peninsula. Quietly he left his mates and worked his way among the gulleys to visit the grave some three miles away, as far as he could judge. The shells were flying over him, both Turkish and British, but he was heedless of them, for a last glance at the resting place, he thought, would bring him close to his old friend. It was not to be. He had proceeded less than two miles on this dangerous journey when he stumbled near the trench of another company. The officer approached and abruptly questioned the lad, who had to acknowledge that it was not part of his orders to be there, but he wanted to see the grave of his pal. " Go back, you idiot," said the officer; " time enough to go up there when you are ordered. We've lost enough already ! " He retraced his steps crestfallen, and blamed his luck for going too near the company whose officer had cut short his little quest for the love of a pal.

That the lads of the 1/5th Bedfordshires bore themselves well and faced the ordeal of a first fight with courage and determination none can doubt. They had to contend with more than the open enemy. A constant daily difficulty was the scarcity of water, which was the enemy above all others, and made the Gallipoli Peninsula a terror to our men, and led to the failure of all efforts put forth by officers and men. Many of the men tell of experiences of thirst which will never be forgotten. The same little allowance of water, which could be easily drunk at a meal, had to serve for washing, shaving, and drinking. Of course, shaving and washing were of minor consideration as a rule. They will tell you of a muddy well which was found, where men sifted the mud out to get a few drops of water, and which they guarded as jealously as if it had been a diamond mine. " What could I do, when my tongue was swollen and refused to keep in my mouth, but drink of the dirty water which my horse enjoys ? " said a young soldier to me. He drank, and the consequence was that the dreadful dysentery seized him.

PRIVATE B. TUFFNELL,
"D" Company, 1/5th Beds. Regt.,
15, York Street, Luton
(*Killed in action at Suvla Bay,
August 15th, 1915*).

PRIVATE A. LLOYD,
1/5th Beds. Regt.,
40, Milton Road, Luton
(*Died of Wounds*).

PRIVATE E. C. PAGE,
1/5th Beds. Regt.,
St. Neots
(*Killed in Action*).

PRIVATE H. F. PUDDEPHATT,
1/5th Beds. Regt.,
50, Butlin Road, Luton
(*Killed in Action*).

It was a sad night for the Bedford boys when they dug themselves in on that fatal 15th of August. Eight of their officers were killed or missing, and the platoons of " A " and " B " Companies had great gaps in them. In all, some 50 non-coms. and men fell in the action, and more than 20 subsequently died of wounds. Many eyes were wet on the evening of that fateful Sunday, and many a soldier lost his best pal. But the battalion, though war worn, is not broken. There still remains the pride of their regiment in them, and their hope is that it will be kept together under their able commander to take its further part in the greatest struggle for liberty which the world has ever seen. And Bedford county says: "All honour to them."

AFTER THE FIGHT.

The lads had put up a good fight and earned the praise of their leaders, but they could not fight the hidden enemy that played such havoc in all the ranks that entered in this unfortunate campaign. Dysentery had broken out among them; strong men were fighting for their very lives—fighting without tools, for the conditions were all in the enemy's favour. Water was only to be got in very limited quantities from the ships, for none was to be found on the Peninsula. No chance to wash, burning heat by day and piercing cold by night, and a good proportion of the lads went under, weakening the battalion and worrying the leaders. It is said that at least a third of the battalion was suffering from dysentery or enteric, and there was very little chance of fighting the evil.

It was a pitiful voyage home for many of them, with the scarcity of nurses and the crowding of the boats. This was war shorn of its glory, and those who saw the conditions of dire helplessness of the victims of the disease will never forget it. Most of them returned home and have found the air of the old

PRIVATE E. PARKER,
  70, Cauldwell Street, Bedford.
PRIVATE A. E. BLAYDON,
  Leagrave.
PRIVATE WILLIAM DIX,
  Flitwick.
PRIVATE G. FARNHAM,
  Eaton Bray.
PRIVATE H. B. CARTER,
  Clifton Road, Shefford.
PRIVATE P. HOWES,
  38, Margetts Road, Kempston.

KILLED IN ACTION.

land the best medicine for the effects of the scourge, but the boats that came over failed to land the sufferers in many cases, and the sea has taken a long toll of the brave hearts from all parts of the Empire who tried to do the impossible in Gallipoli. Many of the Bedfords have thrown off the disease and found their place again in the army. Some of them have been drafted to other regiments, losing the distinction which they prize most—the little " Deer " badge, which shows that they played their part in the ranks of an honoured battalion.

The 1/5th Bedfords retained the position they had won for some days, and then moved to another position at Sari Bahr, and from there were sent on to Alexandria, where they took an active part in operations. They are receiving drafts from the old country, and are getting up to full strength again, and having got acclimatised, they will meet the task which war may demand of them with brave hearts.

> We lay no claim to hero praise,
> Nor dream of deeds in marble writ:
> It is enough if history says
> " They loved their country—did their bit."

PRIVATE C. J. AMBRIDGE,
74, Dane Road, Luton.
PRIVATE C. SNOXELL,
84, Grange Road, Luton.
PRIVATE A. J. ELLINGHAM,
39, Hibbert Street, Luton.

PRIVATE C. R. COUSINS,
47, Chapel Street, Luton.
PRIVATE C. B. BARTON,
18, Brache Street, Luton.
PRIVATE H. BERRY,
Alexandra Avenue, Luton.

KILLED IN ACTION.

In Memoriam.

TWELVE MONTHS LATER.

Tuesday, August 15th, was the anniversary of that fateful day last year fraught with so much anxiety and sorrow to many Luton townspeople. On August 15th, 1915, it will be remembered, what has come to be known as the Battle of Suvla Bay was fought on the Gallipoli Peninsula. The officers and men of the 1/5th Bedfordshire Regiment, called hurriedly into the fighting line, made their memorable advance across the fire-swept zone with a bravery and an intrepidity that was marvellous in new, unseasoned troops. The withering fire of the Turks had a disastrous effect on the advancing Bedfords, but they bravely pressed on, over the rugged and uneven ground, to their objective. This they gained, despite the incessant gun and rifle fire of the enemy. The heroic advance of the Bedfordshire men that day earned for them the soubriquet of "The Yellow Devils." Their deeds secured not only the commendation of the officer commanding, but also evoked the admiration of other regiments who took part in the operations. It was indeed an overwhelming "baptism of fire," but the local men well withstood the shock, and the annals of the regiment had yet brighter lustre inscribed upon them as a result of the gallantry and valour which conferred upon all a new and high distinction on that Eastern battlefield.

HEROISM OF THE BROTHERS PAYNE.

Sergt. Ronald Mc.Cormick, 1/5th Bedfords, whose home is at the "Salisbury Arms," Wellington Street, Luton, writes a graphic account of the experiences of the battalion in the course of a letter to a lady at St. Albans.

He says:—" You will have seen by the papers that we lost a lot of men on that terrible Sunday. I can't make out how I am alive to write this, as shells and

PRIVATE A. SMITH,
 11, Spring Place, Luton.
PRIVATE F. RIMMER,
 153, Tennyson Road, Luton.
PRIVATE ALBERT GRAVES,
 33, York Street, Luton.
PRIVATE A. ANDERSON,
 27, Brache Street, Luton.
KILLED IN ACTION.

bullets were coming all round me. There was only a handful of Bedfords with Capt. Baker, including myself and Albert Payne and Nathan, his brother. We were right in front of the battalion, and Capt. Baker had just given the order to fix our bayonets, when a shell burst and shattered his left arm. He told us to hang on there till he could send more reinforcements up, and Sergt. Payne bound his arm and sent him back with Pte. Findon, who was wounded going back, and Capt. Baker must have been hit again, as he was killed. So we lost one of the best officers who ever donned khaki. We held on as we were ordered for three hours, and then a party of the London Regiment came up with a Capt. Cowley, and over the ridge we went like fury. The Turks did not stop to ask us how we were in health. They ran like the devil, and we shot them as they ran. We took up a position about a thousand yards up this gully from where we started, and we had not been there long before we heard the Turks coming back, and the officer thought they were going to surrender, as they were jabbering to each other and making plenty of noise. He spoke to them in their own language, but had no answer, so he gave us the order to fire, and they fell like corn; but they had got some more men coming round the top of the gully on both sides, and we should have been surrounded, so we on the left were ordered to retire, while those on the right kept up the fire. I managed to get back with several others, but Albert and Nathan Payne must have fallen, as they were on the right, and a land mine went off when we got over the ridge. If Albert had lived I think he would have got something, as he was a hero. All he troubled about was his young brother Nathan."

Pte. F. Smith,
95, High Street, Houghton Regis
(*Killed in Action*).

Private P. Holliman,
300, High Street North, Dunstable
(*Died of Wounds*)

Private G. H. Brown,
27, Cobden Street, Luton
(*Died of Wounds*).

Below are appended the names of men who thus fell gloriously serving their King and Country:—

OFFICERS.

Captain B. C. CUMBERLAND, Luton.
Captain C. T. BAKER, Dunstable.
Captain W. H. MEAKIN, Bedford.
Lieut. F. S. SHOOSMITH, Luton.
Lieut. C. R. LYDEKKER, Harpenden.
Sec.-Lieut. R. D. J. BRIGHTEN, Biggleswade.
Sec.-Lieut. F. RISING, O.B.G.

NON-COMMISSIONED OFFICERS AND MEN.

KILLED.

Sergt. ALBERT PAYNE, Luton.
Sergt. A. HINKS, Luton.
Sergt. W. H. FOSTER, Luton.
Sergt. W. STAPLETON, Ampthill.
Sergt. T. BILLING, Wootton.
Lance-Sergt. A. F. DRACUP.
Lance-Sergt. J. A. W. ROBINSON, Ampthill.
Corpl. NATHAN PAYNE, Luton.
Pte. CHARLES JOHN AMBRIDGE, Luton.
Pte. ALFRED R. COUSINS, Luton.
Pte. C. SNOXELL, Luton.
Pte. CYRIL BERT BARTON, Luton.
Pte. G. H. BROWN, Luton.
Pte. A. J. ELLINGHAM, Luton.
Pte. HAROLD PUDDEPHATT, Luton.
Pte. H. BERRY, Luton.
Pte. A. SMITH, Luton.
Pte. A. GRAVES, Luton.
Pte. B. TUFFNELL, Luton.
Pte. F. RIMMER, Luton.
Pte. A. E. MITCHELL, Luton.
Pte. G. A. V. FINCH, Dunstable.
Pte. FRANK F. FOWLER, Arlesey.
Pte. H. GOODSHIP, Stopsley.
Pte. G. DIEMER, Bedford.
Pte. C. E. PARKER, Bedford.
Pte. G. FARNHAM, Eaton Bray.
Pte. ALBERT EDWARD BLAYDON, Leagrave.
Pte. H. B. CARTER, Shefford.
Pte. WM. DIX, Flitwick.
Pte. E. C. PAGE, St. Neots.
Pte. G. HUTCHINGS.
Pte. M. SHREEVES.
Pte. E. J. CAVES.

The Story of the First-Fifth Bedfords. 79

Pte. P. HOWES, Kempston.
Pte. E. OVERTON.
Pte. E. ANDERSON.
Pte. SEABROOK, Dunstable.

DIED OF WOUNDS.

Sergt. T. BUTLER, Wootton.
Corpl. WM. JARVIS, Luton.
Lance-Corpl. ROWLAND ABBOTT, Luton.
Pte. L. HURD, Luton.
Pte. JAMES STENHOUSE, Luton.
Pte. H. BARTON, Luton.
Pte. F. W. THURLOW, Luton.
Pte. H. MARDLE, Caddington.
Pte. E. G. PAGE, St. Neots.
Pte. A. J. CURTIS, Bromham.
Pte. A. WOODCRAFT, Flitwick.
Pte. G. STOKES, Kempston.
Pte. C. A. SMITH.
Pte. G. BROWN.
Pte. W. J. MAYNARD.
Pte. W. J. BAKER.
Pte. W. J. FLORIN.
Pte. H. ROBINSON.
Pte. P. HOLLIMAN.
Pte. A. LAWSON.
Pte. H. QUICK, Leighton Buzzard.
Pte. A. LLOYD.

In addition to the above, there were a considerable number wounded in the action, and many were stricken with dysentery.

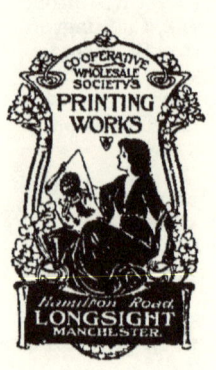

www.ingramcontent.com/pod-product-compliance
Lightning Source LLC
Chambersburg PA
CBHW032133090426
42743CB00007B/587